SAS ANTI-SURVEILLANCE AND COUNTER-SURVEILLANCE TECHNIQUES

VARANGIAN PRESS

ISBN:10:1983409057
ISBN-13:978-1983409059

INFATUO MODO DISCIT AB EXPERIENTIA

"A fool learns only from experience"

CONTENTS

BRIEF HISTORY OF THE ASASR

The SASR can trace its beginnings back to the Australian Z Special Unit and Independent Commando Companies that fought during the Second World War. On 25 July 1957, the 1st Special Air Service Company, Royal Australian Infantry, was raised at Campbell Barracks, Swanbourne, in Western Australia; largely modelled on the British SAS.

"The Company consisted of a headquarters and four platoons comprising about 200 all ranks by the time it became part of The Royal Australian Regiment in 1960." At the same time it was given responsibility for commando and SF operations in the Australian Army.

On 04 September 1964, the 1st Special Air Service Company was expanded to become the Special Air Service Regiment with three sabre squadrons. Following disengagement from Vietnam in October 1971, 2 Squadron was disbanded to allow the SAS Training Squadron to be raised (later renamed the SAS Support Squadron, subsequently the Operational Support Squadron).

The SASR gained its CT remit on 23 February 1978 after a terrorist attack on the Sydney Hilton on the 13 February in the same year. In order to maintain the SASRs CT and war role capabilities, in 1982 the disbanded 2 Squadron was reformed.

CHAPTER 1

IDENTIFYING SURVEILLANCE

DEFINITIONS

ANTI-SURVEILLANCE:

Employing Techniques To Evade Surveillance

COUNTER-SURVEILLANCE:

The discreet application of techniques used to identify and contain surveillance by:

- Detection
- Identification
- Revision of Activity

THOSE ACTIONS SHOULD BE DISCRETE SO AS NOT TO CONFIRM THAT COUNTER-SURVEILLANCE TECHNIQUES ARE BEING UTILISED.

INTRODUCTION

Counter-surveillance and anti-surveillance, particularly with respect to operators, must be considered from two aspects:

•As conducted by a subject of surveillance

•As practiced by a Surveillance Operator

The object of this document is to make the operator aware of some counter- surveillance techniques. These can and have been employed by foreign sources and hostile intelligence officers during the course of their activities, or by a surveillance operator to protect their own operational and personal security.

When conducting surveillance of a potential source, it is important that an officer is able to recognise when a subject is employing counter or anti-surveillance techniques. Besides the immediate risks such activities pose to an operation, the application of CS or AS can suggest a higher level of sophistication and/or training of the potential source. This can then have a flow-on effect to other aspects of an operation such as identification of potential double-agents.

Operators should also practice counter-surveillance as part of their operational routine. They may need to conduct counter-surveillance to confirm surveillance by a foreign intelligence service directed at the officer, or simply to maintain OPSEC or security for official or private premises.

In general, surveillance involves the observation of a specific person, object or place. Most people who would place you under surveillance are well-skilled at such an activity. Most likely, any attempt would be professionally conducted with the use of vehicles and as many as twenty surveillance operators plus their support personnel. However, the routine use of even basic counter-surveillance drills can thwart or mislead a Foreign intelligence service. The experience of finding or suspecting that you are under surveillance can be traumatic or at least stressful, but as expected, it comes with the territory.

The application of the measures outlined in this document cannot guarantee that an operator will not successfully be placed under surveillance by a foreign intelligence service. However, the prudent and careful application of the commonsense measures which are outlined in this document will enable you to detect or even deter even a professional and well-planned surveillance operation.

Consider whether your current duties or operational commitments dictate the use of anti or counter-surveillance, based on operational information available and immediate circumstances. There may instances when you are required to employ constant counter-surveillance for your own operational security.

There are basically three forms of surveillance: foot, vehicle, and stationary (generally categorized as either mobile or static). A brief description of the most common techniques used for each of these forms and methods for detecting each one follows in the next section.

IDENTIFYING SURVEILLANCE

THE RECONNAISSANCE

Before undertaking surveillance most experts gather information about the subject from other sources. Records of information made available to the threat organization from a sympathetic individual within an organization, local police, or other government office may reveal useful facts about an individual such as the names of family members, an address, a description of vehicles and license numbers, photographs, etc. The surveillance operators will also make a reconnaissance of the neighbourhoods in which the target lives and works. This permits them to select positions of observation, the types of vehicles to use, the clothing to be worn, and the type of ruse to use that will give them an ordinary or normal appearance and plausible reasons to be in the area.

FOOT SURVEILLANCE

The following common sense considerations will help to increase the possibility of detecting foot surveillance.

One or more individuals may undertake foot surveillance. One-person foot surveillance is rather complicated and fairly easy to detect. The surveillance operator must remain close to the target, particularly in congested areas, to avoid losing him or her.

In less congested areas the surveillance operator can maintain a greater distance, but the lack of other pedestrians makes the surveillance operator that much more noticeable.

The one complicating factor is the use of a disguise to make the surveillance operator look different (perhaps a uniform). One possible use of a disguise is a shopping bag or some other container for a change of clothes, particularly if the shopping bag is from a store not found in the area or the container somehow seems out of place. Where a disguise is suspected, pay particular attention to shoes and slacks or skirts. These items are less easily and, therefore, less commonly changed.

In elevators, watch for people who seem to wait for you to push a button and then select a floor one flight above or below yours.

Two-person foot surveillance is more effective in that the second surveillance operator provides greater flexibility. Normally, one surveillance operator remains close to the target while the other stays at a greater distance. The second surveillance operator may follow the first on the same side of the street or travel on the opposite side. Periodically the two surveillance operators change position so that if the target spots one of them, that one will soon be out of sight, leading the target to think that he or she was mistaken. Obviously, spotting this form of surveillance is more complicated, but individuals who are alert to the people in their vicinity will eventually detect the same surveillance operator over a period of time.

Foot surveillance with three or more people uses the most sophisticated techniques and is the most difficult to spot. Generally, one surveillance operator remains behind the target close enough to respond to any sudden moves.

A second surveillance operator remains behind the first on the same side of the street with the first surveillance operator in sight.

A third surveillance operator travels on the opposite side of the street parallel with or just behind the target. In areas where the target has few paths to choose, one surveillance operator may walk in front of the target, where he or she is least likely to cause suspicion. The positions of the surveillance operators are frequently changed, most commonly at intersections.

The surveillance operator directly behind the target may move to the opposite side of the street, while another surveillance operator moves in close behind the target. With the additional surveillance operators, any operator who feels that he or she has been observed may drop out of the formation.

The use of this sophisticated technique requires that people be alert not only to those people behind them but also to those across the street and perhaps in front of them. If the same person is seen more than once over a certain distance, surveillance may be suspected even if that person is not continuously seen.

Common methods for detecting surveillance apply to all three forms of foot surveillance. The most effective are:

•Stopping abruptly and looking to the rear,

•Suddenly reversing your course,

•Stopping abruptly after turning a corner,

•Watching reflections in shop windows or other reflective surfaces,

•Entering a building and leaving immediately by another exit,

•Walking slowly and then rapidly at intervals,

•Dropping a piece of paper to see if anyone retrieves it,

Boarding or exiting a bus or subway just before it starts, and

•Making sudden turns or walking around the block.

While taking these actions, watch for people who are taken by surprise, react inappropriately, suddenly change direction, or give a signal to someone else.

Surveillance operators will not normally look directly at the target, but they may do so if they are surprised or unaware that you are observing them.

In particular, look for people:

•Peering over crowds

•Rubber neck / swivel head

•Peering around corners

•Using reflections

•Abruptly exiting premises

•Whose mannerisms indicate nervousness or stress

•Who continually appear in the area, shop, building, etc. that you are visiting (common sense dictates that you should not focus on persons who have a legitimate reason to be in the area – workers, employees, etc.)

•Who do not appear to have a purpose or who are loitering

•Who avoid eye contact with you (while this reaction is not uncommon, it may, with other indicators, enable you to identify a surveillance effort).

•Who are not dressed appropriately for the locality (inappropriate clothing for location or weather conditions, a suit and tie amid casually-dressed people or vice-versa, etc).

•Who appear to be wearing obvious disguises (false hair, moustache, etc.).

Running or moving very quickly in your direction or in the direction of your intended destination.

•Making short notes in pads or folders.

•Using a personal recorder

•Taking photographs of you.

•Utilising communications equipment (including phones).

NOTE: Do not take any ONE of the above indicators as confirmation that you are under surveillance. Look for a number of indicators and, if necessary, test for surveillance.

Once you have confirmed that you are under surveillance, you should consider your actions. Always contact the Security Advisor for the Station in question. If practicable, then commence anti-surveillance techniques illustrated later in this document.

VEHICLE SURVEILLANCE

As with foot surveillance, vehicle surveillance may be undertaken using only one vehicle or using two or more vehicles. One-vehicle surveillance suffers from the same drawbacks as one-person foot surveillance. The target has to be kept in view at all times and followed by the same vehicle. Surveillance operators can try to overcome this advantage somewhat by changing seating arrangements within the vehicle; putting on and taking off hats, coats, and sunglasses; changing license plates; and turning off onto side streets and then turning back to resume the tail. This makes it necessary for a person suspecting surveillance to remember aspects of a following vehicle that cannot easily be changed such as the make, model, and colour of the car and any body damage such as rust, dents, etc.

The use of two or more vehicles permits surveillance operators to switch positions or to drop out of the surveillance when necessary. One vehicle follows the target vehicle and directs other vehicles by radio.

The other vehicle may follow behind the lead surveillance vehicle, precede the target vehicle, or travel on parallel roads. At intersections, the vehicle following directly behind the target vehicle will generally travel straight ahead while alerting all other vehicles of the direction in which the target vehicle has turned. Another vehicle in the formation will then take a position behind the target and become the lead vehicle, taking over the responsibility for giving instructions to other surveillance operators. The former lead vehicle then makes a U-turn or travels around the block to take up a new position ready to resume the lead vehicle position again when necessary.

People who have well established routines permit surveillance operators to use methods that are much more difficult to detect. If, for example, you leave the office at the same time each day and travel by the most direct route to your home or if you live in a remote area with a few or no alternate routes to your home, surveillance operators have no need to follow you all the way to your residence. An alternative method of surveillance in such situations is leading surveillance and progressive surveillance.

In leading surveillance the surveillance operator travels in front of the target while the observer watches for turns. When the target turns, this is noted. The next day the surveillance operator makes a turn where the target did the previous day. Over a period of time the surveillance operators will discover the entire route to the residence while still driving in a position that creates much less suspicion.

There are two forms of progressive surveillance. In the first form, surveillance operators are placed at intersections along the probable routes of the target. When the target makes a turn, this is noted and the position of the surveillance operators is adjusted to check the next intersection. Eventually, this method leads the surveillance operators to the residence.

In the second form or progressive surveillance, a vehicle will follow the target for a short distance and then turn off. On successive days the surveillance operator picks up the target where he or she left off the previous day. Leading and progressive surveillance are extremely difficult to detect, but you should not give anyone the opportunity to use these methods.

Vehicle surveillance is a very difficult operation to carry out successfully without detection.

To help identify vehicle surveillance:

•Be alert for strangers or unusual cars at the start of a journey.

•Note vehicles which are not familiar in your street or area.

•Note and closely observe any vehicle which consistently drives too close or maintains an excessive distance behind your vehicle.

•Note any vehicles that behave in an erratic manner (change lanes frequently, run red lights and stop signs, etc.)

•Observe and make a mental note of any vehicles that change direction with you.

•Drive slower than the flow of traffic and observe for vehicles doing the same.

Concentrate on observing vehicles parking and departing at the same times as you.

•Vehicles which do not indicate when changing lanes or turning corners.

•Stop in a sparsely settled area to see if anyone else stops.

Drive up a dead-end street to see if anyone is following. If not, stop and exit the vehicle momentarily, then re-enter and drive out of the street again. Do a quick

U-turn, then repeat the procedure, looking for the same vehicles parked in an overwatch position of the entrance to the street.

The most effective methods for detecting most forms of vehicle surveillance are:

1.Making a U-turn where it is safe to do so,

2.Making a turn to the right or left (in general, right turns create greater complications for surveillance operators because of oncoming traffic that may delay a turn),

3.Going through a traffic light just as it is turning red,

4.Stopping just beyond a curve or hill, and

5.Circling a block.

In each case, watch for the reactions of any vehicles that you may suspect. Any vehicles that make unusual manoeuvres should be carefully noted. Do not forget to check for motorcycles or motorbikes, since in many parts of the world they seem to be favoured by surveillance operators because they move easily through heavy traffic.

COMBINED FOOT/VEHICLE SURVEILLANCE

Foot surveillance is often used in conjunction with vehicle surveillance since it is likely that the target will use a combination of foot and vehicle transportation.

Vehicles used for surveillance are inconspicuous in appearance and of a subdued colour. Frequently, the inside dome light is made inoperative so that it will not illuminate the interior of the car when the door is opened. Vehicles will have two or more people in them so that if the target parks his or her vehicle and walks away, the surveillance can be resumed on foot while the driver remains with the vehicle. While moving, the driver gives full attention to driving while the observer operates the radio, watches the target, and makes notes on the target's activities.

Sometimes it will be necessary for surveillance operators to break traffic regulations to avoid losing you. If you see a vehicle run a red light, make an illegal U-turn, travel over the speed limit, or make dangerous or sudden lane changes in an apparent effort to keep up with you, you should, of course, be suspicious of that vehicle. The distance between a surveillance vehicle and the target will vary depending on the speed at which the vehicles are travelling and the amount of traffic. Surveillance operators will try to keep one or two vehicles between themselves and the target.

STATIC SURVEILLANCE

Static surveillance is commonly used by terrorist and criminal organizations. Most surveillance targets are acquired by the surveillance team near the residence or office because that part of the route is least easily varied. Most people are more vulnerable in the morning when departing for work, because morning departure times are more predictable than are evening arrivals.

Surveillance operators seek a position that permits them to observe the residence or office clearly without being observed or suspected. Surveillance operators want to identify observation points that afford the best view of the target. Foot and vehicular traffic, buildings and terrain around each government facility vary with each location. Pedestrian traffic, rush hour traffic flow, temporary street closure, etc. will affect observation points.

If the surveillance operators decide that it is best not to be seen, they may obtain an apartment or rent office space in the area that provides for an adequate view, but such apartments or office space may not be available and the renting of an apartment or office space could provide clues for a subsequent investigation.

The use of an apartment or office space for surveillance, while possibly the most difficult to detect, is generally not the easiest or safest method. Many surveillance teams use vans with windows in the side or back that permit observation from the interior of the van. Often the van will have the name of a store or utility company to provide some pretext for its being in the area. The driver may park the van and walk away, leaving the surveillance team inside. Some teams use sedans for stationary surveillance, parking the vehicle far enough from the residence or office to be less noticeable, using other vehicles for cover, facing the vehicle away from the target, and using the rear view mirrors to watch.

Where it is not possible to watch the residence or office unobserved, surveillance operators must come up with a plausible reason for being in the area. The types of ruses used are limited only by the surveillance operator's imagination. Some of the more commonly used covers are automotive repairs due to engine trouble or a flat tire, door to door sales, utility repair crews, lovers in a park, construction work, or sitting at a cafe. Women, children and dogs are often used to give a greater appearance of innocence.

Some things to check for are parked vehicles with people in them, cars with more mirrors or mirrors that are larger than normal, people seen in the area more frequently than seems normal, people who are dressed inappropriately, and workers who seem to accomplish nothing.

If you become suspicious of a van, note any information printed on the side of the van, including telephone numbers. Check the telephone book or relevant databases to see if such a business exists. Note the license numbers of any suspicious vehicles and provide them to your security adviser so they can be checked.

POINTS OF VULNERABILITY

Pay particular attention to your observation and counter-surveillance skills at points where surveillance may commence on you;

•Place of work

•Place of residence

•Places frequented during operations (motels, airports and other premises utilised)

•Your vehicles

Be mindful that previous operations may compromise these locations or operational information may become available to others.

AREA FAMILIARISATION

Area familiarity, or at least the lack of it, is probably the cause of more operational target losses than any other. Unfortunately, operators concerned do not always acknowledge this. If the causes of target losses were looked at in detail, lack of area familiarity would almost always be the single over-riding factor. A good knowledge of the area in which a target operates will, in many cases, prevent a loss no matter what other difficulties occur.

This should be considered where officers are endeavouring to perform counter surveillance.

Area familiarisation knowledge will assist in determining where surveillance may be situated or commenced and also assist in allowing officers to concentrate on observations rather than directions and navigation.

Primary Knowledge

•Suburbs – location, names, socioeconomic composition and nationalities.

•Traffic systems – Major streets, arterial roads, expressways, traffic flow, parking restrictions.

•Designated and recurring points – Major shopping centres and malls, hotels, entertainment and tourist areas.

•Public transport – Transport terminals, airports, railway and bus interchanges, taxi ranks and depots.

•Areas of interest – Restaurants, art galleries, libraries, landmarks and monuments of interest to tourists.

•Accommodation – Hotels, motels, caravan parks, resorts and bed & breakfasts.

Secondary Knowledge

This relates to the need for special attention concerning the location and layout of points of interest for a surveillance team.

•Suburbs – Types of vehicles, cover in streets (e.g. a surveillance vehicle will almost always "stack" near a high fence or wall if possible when waiting to respond in a surrounding street), local shops and facilities (toilets with easy access within a 1-2 km radius), entry and exit from the suburb, occupation and "no-go" areas.

•Traffic systems – Names of streets, intersections, parallels, access routes, traffic conditions at various times, traffic lights and phasing, timings, one- way streets.

•Designated and recurring points – Entry/exit points, shops, banks, ATMs, eating areas

•Public transport – Route numbers and frequency, destinations, costs, timings

•Areas of interest – Entry/exit, parking, hours of access, cost, phones, toilets, security, stairs, lifts, escalators, tenants.

•Accommodation – Entry and exits, type and rating, cost, dress code, security, parking, bars and restaurants.

Thorough area knowledge cannot be stressed enough. When conducting counter-surveillance in a specific area every effort should be made to carry out a thorough survey of the area prior to commencing the operation. The surveillance team may have personal knowledge of the area through past operations or the area being home for one or more members of the surveillance team.

Area Familiarisation Golden Rules

•Always increase area familiarisation (including out of hours)

•Study the "innocent man" in each area and try to copy him/her

•Learn about surveillance methods

•Plan in down time

IN ANY MILITARY OPERATION, IT IS IMPORTANT FIRST

TO KNOW THE LAY OF THE LAND

Sun Tzu 500BC

CHAPTER 2

ANTI-SURVEILLANCE

Techniques employed to evade surveillance:

ON FOOT

During a suspected foot surveillance, consider the following options -

•Turning a corner and stopping or walking back.

•Reversing direction of travel at any point.

•Using escalators and lifts and stopping at the top.

•Public Transport – Being last to board, waiting until the vehicle is about to leave and getting off, getting off at the first stop or an isolated stop.

•Leaving a building through a side door or rarely used exit.

•Stopping a passing taxi when there are no others in sight.

•Mingling with crowds in a store.

•Changing your appearance.

IN VEHICLES

•Running traffic lights.(emergency use)

•U turns.

•Alternatively driving slowly then quickly.

•Driving slowly for a long period of time.

•Driving against traffic in one way streets (emergency use)

•Driving into dead-end streets and cul de sacs.

•Driving quickly, then stopping in a blind location to observe other vehicles come past at speed.

•Driving around the block from the suspected surveillance start point.

•Driving into and straight out of a parking area.

•Turning without indicating or turning a corner from the wrong lane.

Consider the advantage of conducting anti-surveillance out of sight of the surveillance team.

CHAPTER 3

COUNTER SURVEILLANCE TECHNIQUES

Counter surveillance is the application of techniques to identify and counteract possible surveillance. This is done in three stages:

•Detect

•Identify

•Revise activity or continue

Do not let your actions confirm counter surveillance.

ON FOOT

To counter suspected foot surveillance consider the following options:

•Walking along "corridors".

•Walking through "choke points".

•"Towing" the surveillance team around.

•Walking along streets with little cover.

•Using a support person to assist in the detection of surveillance.

•Use area familiarisation to advantage.

•Use window reflections.

•Make a mental note of suspected persons and look for reappearance at other locations.

•Drop an object, walk on, then observe who approaches the object.

Testing for surveillance may be accomplished by any or a combination of the following means:

•Stopping suddenly and observing for a similar action.

•Boarding public transport and observing any people who board with or after you.

•Leaving public transport and observing who exits with you.

•Varying walking speed and observe who follows the pattern.

•Stopping around a corner and observing who follows.

•Making a mental note of persons of interest and look for reappearance at other locations.

•Seeing the same face three times in three different areas is a reliable indicator that surveillance has commenced.

IN VEHICLES

•Using "corridors" and "choke points".

•Stopping to check road map and noting vehicles that pass.

•Stopping due to "engine problems" and noting vehicles which pass.

•Use a support person to observe for indicators or suspicious activity.

•Avoiding regular arrival and departure times.

•Varying the route you take when traveling to common destinations.

•Stopping suddenly and after the suspected vehicle has passed drive in the opposite direction (emergency use only).

There are variations on the methods listed above and many more. Counter surveillance is only limited by the ingenuity of the target. One advantage of using counter surveillance techniques is that when a team member is burned, they will be withdrawn from the surveillance operation, severely limiting the capabilities of the surveillance team. If the team is compromised, it will generally be withdrawn and surveillance ceased, but beware of a second unseen surveillance team (the FBI decoy team method).

REMEMBER

•Act routinely, even bored.

•Slow, not fast.

•Try to draw the surveillance team toward you to isolate and identify team members.

Walking around is not effective. Use parks and other open spaces to:

•Isolate surveillance team members.

•Use support personnel to observe for surveillance activity.

•Counter surveillance tactics should appear innocent and indiscernible from normal activities.

COUNTER SURVEILLANCE CYCLE AND PLANNING

It is not paranoid or gung-ho to conduct a "dry-cleaning" operation before returning to station, meeting a source or even returning home. It is a standard operating procedure.

To perform counter surveillance successfully, planning should be conducted where possible. Consider the use of the counter surveillance cycle coupled with planning of routes and location of checking zones to maximise efforts to identify surveillance.

In planning for the counter surveillance cycle consider the following:

•Use of unparalled roads and "choke points"

•Quiet/one way streets.

•Use of support personnel.

•Public transport.

•Sparsely populated areas.

•Subtle changes of speed.

•Rear vision mirrors.

CHECKING ZONES

Choose areas in which to check for surveillance indicators. Generally these areas include "corridors" and "choke points" for both vehicle and foot surveillance and public transport.

"DRY-CLEANING" ZONES

These are areas where surveillance would be difficult to conduct. Generally areas classified as "spaces" and heavy traffic areas. Using area familiarisation knowledge will assist is "dry cleaning" (e.g. Premises with unlikely exits, both vehicular and foot).

Once you have established a route that will give advantages in identifying surveillance, utilise the following methods:

•Stopping suddenly.

•Subtle changes of speed.

•Rear vision mirrors.

CHECKING ZONES

Choose areas in which to check for surveillance indicators. Generally these areas include "corridors" and "choke points" for both vehicle and foot surveillance and public transport.

"DRY-CLEANING" ZONES

These are areas where surveillance would be difficult to conduct. Generally areas classified as "spaces" and heavy traffic areas. Using area familiarisation knowledge will assist is "dry cleaning" (e.g. Premises with unlikely exits, both vehicular and foot).

Once you have established a route that will give advantages in identifying surveillance, utilise the following methods:

•Stopping suddenly.

•Subtle changes of speed.

•Park and walk some distance to locations.

•Rear vision mirrors.

•Slow on highways/freeways.

•Phone box/lost/car trouble

•Support personnel as observers.

REMEMBER:

Basic rules –

•Plan the route

•Act naturally

•Look the part

•Act with a purpose

•Use area familiarisation

•Have a logical cover story

Do Not –

•Establish a pattern

•Let your actions confirm counter surveillance

Continual planning is required. Hostile surveillance is simplified if a target adopts a pattern of conduct or frequents the same locations on a regular basis.

USE OF SUPPORT PERSONNEL

The use of support personnel to assist with planning, counter surveillance, survey of premises and routes as well as close protection should be considered.

A possible scenario for a three-person team may be:

•All plan the route and venues for operations and conduct surveys of premises likely to be visited or utilised for operations.

•All travel to a location where the subject of the operation will meet two members of the team. This location should also be considered in planning.

CONDUCT THE COUNTER SURVEILLANCE CYCLE FROM THE STATION TO THE OPERATIONAL LOCATION. AS A GENERAL RULE, AVOID MEETING A SUBJECT ON HOME TURF.

•Two members of the team meet the subject. The support member oversights the meeting and checks for surveillance indicators.

•Two members depart the location with the source, possibly using a taxi or other public transport which hostile surveillance will not have previously identified. Indicate to the driver the route to be taken.

•A support member checks for surveillance at "choke points" along the route, then travels to the location to check for physical security threats and to clear it.

•Pair with source makes phone contact with the support officer to check all clear.

•Support member oversights the arrival of the pair and the source, then checks the surrounding area for hostile surveillance.

•Contact concludes and the source is returned to the point of pick up. Once again, the support member conducts counter surveillance.

•At no time should the support member acknowledge the pair and communications between them should be discrete and secure. Ensure locations for drop-off and pick-up of pair by the support member are chosen based on knowledge of surveillance practices.

The basic principles outlined above may be adapted for use by a two person team, however other operational considerations may determine operational methods (e.g. The need for corroboration of conversation with the source, personal security, etc.)

Prior planning in the selection of and survey of premises to be utilised for contacts is of prime importance to the success of operations.

Planning in down time will assist during future operations. This allows for the selection of a location at short notice. The completion of a formal survey and reconnaissance to maintained on file should be considered.

During the selection of premises, consider the following:

•General location, taking into consideration topography and other surveillance considerations.

•Escape routes from the area.

•Entry and exit points from the premises.

•Locate possible hostile surveillance OP points and stacks.

CONCLUSION

Make a habit of checking the neighbourhood through a window before you go out each day.

Detecting surveillance requires a constant state of alertness and must become an unconscious habit. We do not want to encourage paranoia, but a good sense of what is normal and what is unusual in your surroundings could be more important than any other type of security precaution you take. Above all, do not hesitate to report any unusual events.